Searchlight
BOOKS™

Space Mysteries

Mysteries of the

Moon

Rebecca E. Hirsch

Lerner Publications ◆ Minneapolis

Lerner Publications Company
An imprint of Lerner Publishing Group, Inc.
241 First Avenue North
Minneapolis, MN 55401 USA

For reading levels and more information, look up this title
at www.lernerbooks.com.

Main body text set in Adrianna Regular 14/20.
Typeface provided by Chank.

Designer: Mary Ross

Library of Congress Cataloging-in-Publication Data

Names: Hirsch, Rebecca E., author.
Title: Mysteries of the moon / Rebecca E. Hirsch.
Other titles: Searchlight books. Space mysteries.
Description: Minneapolis : Lerner Publications, [2021] | Series: Searchlight books —
    space mysteries | Includes bibliographical references and index. | Audience: Ages
    8–11 | Audience: Grades 2–3 | Summary: "Where did the moon come from? And
    what could be hiding on its dark side? Young readers can learn about the current
    mysteries surrounding the moon"— Provided by publisher.
Identifiers: LCCN 2019055130 (print) | LCCN 2019055131
    (ebook) | ISBN 9781541597396 (library binding) | ISBN 9781728413891 (paperback) |
    ISBN 9781728400907 (ebook)
Subjects: LCSH: Moon—Juvenile literature.
Classification: LCC QB582 .H57 2021 (print) | LCC QB582 (ebook) | DDC 523.3—dc23

LC record available at https://lccn.loc.gov/2019055130
LC ebook record available at https://lccn.loc.gov/2019055131

Manufactured in the United States of America
1-47843-48283-2/26/2020

Contents

Chapter 1

MEET THE MOON

Look up at the sky on a clear night. You might see the moon shining brightly. The moon is a ball of rock that orbits Earth. It is the closest space object to our planet. The moon is very different from our planet, though. It has no air, and it's covered in dust. Nothing can live on the moon.

The moon is the biggest and brightest object in the night sky.

AN ASTRONAUT JUMPS ABOVE THE MOON'S
SURFACE IN 1972. THE MOON'S LOW
GRAVITY MADE IT EASIER TO JUMP HIGH.

▼

The moon is about four times smaller than Earth.
Because it is smaller, it has less gravity. Suppose you
visited the moon. With less gravity pulling you toward the
ground, you'd be much lighter. If you weigh 100 pounds
(45 kg) on Earth, you would weigh just 16.5 pounds (7.5 kg)
on the moon.

Moonlight

The moon shines brightly, but it doesn't make its own light. The moon reflects light from the sun.

When we look at the moon from Earth, it appears to change shape night after night. But the shape doesn't really change. What changes is our view. We see different parts of the moon as the sun shines on different parts of its surface. These different views are phases.

During the new moon phase, the moon looks dark. The sun lights up the side of the moon that faces away from Earth. The side facing us is in shadow. After a new moon, the sun starts to light up the side that faces Earth. The sunlit part grows bigger each night. After about two weeks, the sun completely lights up the side of the moon that faces Earth. This is a full moon. It looks big, round, and bright. After that, the sunlit part grows smaller. We see less of the moon each night. The cycle ends with another new moon. The whole cycle takes about one month.

The sun lights up half of the moon in this photo.

Missions to the Moon

People have wondered about the moon since ancient times. Scientists in the past drew pictures of the moon's changing shape. They made calendars based on its phases. In the seventeenth century, people began to look at the moon with telescopes.

In the 1950s, people started to explore the moon with spacecraft. Some spacecraft flew around the moon and took pictures. Other spacecraft landed on the moon's surface.

This chart, made around 1450 in the Middle East, shows the moon's phases.

In 1969, the United States sent astronauts to the moon. The astronauts were the first people ever to walk on the moon. They carried oxygen tanks so they could breathe.

US astronauts made four more trips to the moon in the early 1970s. They took pictures and collected moon rocks and soil. They left American flags, moon buggies, and other equipment on the moon. The moon is the only place outside of Earth that people have ever visited.

Astronaut Buzz Aldrin was on the first mission to the moon.

After the astronauts visited, the United States, the Soviet Union (a union of republics that included Russia), China, and other nations sent unpiloted spacecraft to the moon. Some spacecraft orbited the moon. They took measurements, made maps, and photographed the moon from space. Other spacecraft landed on the moon. They carried scientific instruments to test the moon's soil, gases, and other substances.

THIS CHINESE SPACECRAFT LANDED ON THE MOON IN 2019.

STEM Spotlight

On three missions, astronauts rode moon buggies across the moon. Each buggy could hold two astronauts. It carried communication gear and scientific equipment. Each buggy's top speed was 8 miles (13 km) per hour. The astronauts drove only a few miles from their base. That way, if the buggy broke down, the astronauts could walk back to base. The astronauts left the buggies on the moon when they went back to Earth.

Chapter 2

BIRTH OF THE MOON

Where did the moon come from? Scientists think that about 4.5 billion years ago, a planet called Theia smashed into Earth. Theia was about as big as Mars. During the crash, a cloud of rock, dust, and gases shot off into space. Gravity pulled some of this material together into a ball. That ball was the moon.

An illustration shows Theia smashing into Earth.

The details of the ancient collision are mysterious. Perhaps, when the two planets smashed together, Theia broke into pieces, but Earth did not break apart. If that happened, then the debris that shot out into space and formed the moon was made of only Theia.

Another idea is that both planets broke apart during the collision. Afterward, the debris from the two planets mixed together. Most of the debris clumped together to form a new Earth. A smaller portion of the debris formed the moon.

Astronauts scooped up soil and rocks from the moon. These samples help scientists figure out how the moon formed.

A Fiery Blast

To find out what happened, scientists have looked for answers in moon rocks. They have compared rocks found on Earth to ones that astronauts brought back from the moon. They discovered that moon rocks are made of the same materials as rocks from inside Earth.

Based on that evidence, scientists think that both Theia and Earth exploded in the ancient collision. The debris from the two planets then mixed together. Both Earth and the moon are made from this mixture.

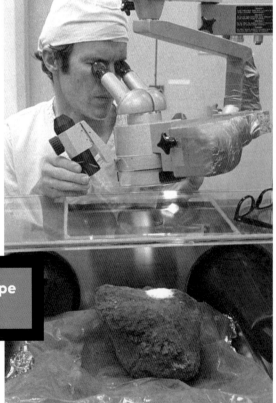

A scientist uses a microscope to study a moon rock.

TWO SIDES OF THE MOON

The moon moves in two ways. It orbits Earth, and it also rotates, or spins, on its axis. One full trip around Earth takes the moon twenty-nine and a half days. One full spin around its axis also takes the moon twenty-nine and a half days. Because the orbit and the rotation take the same amount of time, one side of the moon always faces Earth. The other side always faces away.

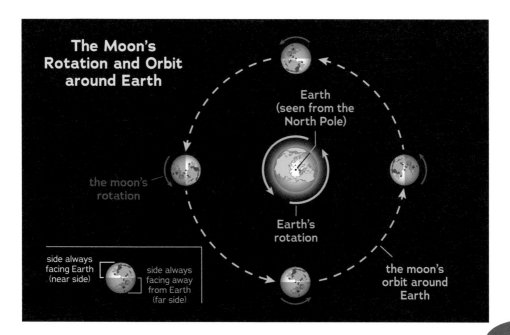

The Moon's Rotation and Orbit around Earth

Earth (seen from the North Pole)

the moon's rotation

Earth's rotation

side always facing Earth (near side)

side always facing away from Earth (far side)

the moon's orbit around Earth

The side of the moon that faces Earth is called the near side. The side that faces away is the far side. For thousands of years, no one knew what the far side looked like. In 1959, *Luna 3*, a spacecraft from the Soviet Union, flew by the far side of the moon and took pictures.

This photograph of the far side of the moon shows its many craters.

Spacecraft have taken close-up photographs of craters on the moon.

Photographs from *Luna 3* and other spacecraft show that the far side is covered with craters and mountains. The craters formed when asteroids struck the moon, threw up debris, and left deep pits.

The near side has craters too. But it also has vast dark plains called maria. *Maria* means "seas" in Latin, but maria aren't made of water. They are made of rock. Millions of years ago, hot lava from deep inside the moon shot up to the surface through volcanoes. The lava ran over the surface, cooled down, and hardened into rock.

Molten Moon

Using seismographs and other instruments, scientists have discovered that the crust on the far side of the moon is twice as thick as the crust of the near side. Why is the crust thicker on one side than the other? Why does only the near side have maria?

The answers may come from the collision between Earth and Theia. It was a hot, violent crash. It heated Earth to a temperature of more than 4,500°F (2,500°C).

Dark, flat areas on the moon's surface are called maria.

Heat from Earth made the moon hot too. Because it always faced Earth, the near side was hotter. The far side of the moon did not get as much of Earth's heat. So that side cooled more quickly. As it cooled, its outer layer hardened into a thick crust. On the near side, the outer layer stayed hot longer. When that side cooled, the outer layer formed a thinner crust.

On the near side, hot lava easily shot through the thin crust to form maria. But on the far side, the thick crust blocked the lava flows. So no maria formed.

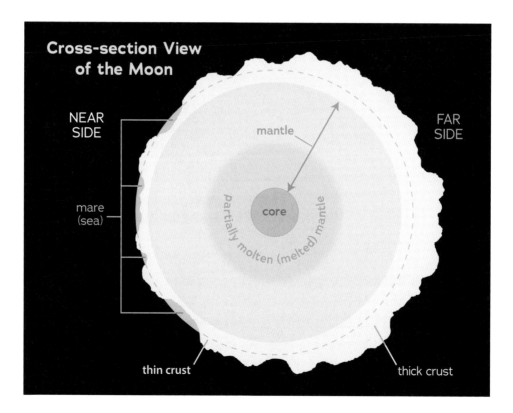

Cross-section View of the Moon

NEAR SIDE

FAR SIDE

mantle

mare (sea)

Partially molten (melted) mantle

core

thin crust

thick crust

Space Fact or Fiction?

The far side of the moon is in darkness all the time.

This is fiction. People sometimes describe the far side of the moon as the dark side. We cannot see this side from Earth, but it is not always dark. As the moon rotates, the far side gets just as much sunlight and darkness as the near side.

Chapter 4

MOON SECRETS

Scientists once thought the moon was completely dry. But in the twenty-first century, scientists looked closer at moon rocks collected by astronauts many years before. Scientists discovered that the rocks contained tiny amounts of water. In 2008, an Indian spacecraft carried scientific instruments to the moon. The instruments found frozen water mixed into the moon's soil on some parts of the moon.

This is a model of the Indian spacecraft that discovered water on the moon.

How much water is on the moon? In 2022, the US National Aeronautics and Space Administration (NASA) will send a spacecraft to find out. The *VIPER* lunar rover will explore the moon's south pole and test for ice there. *VIPER* will create a map showing the location and thickness of the ice.

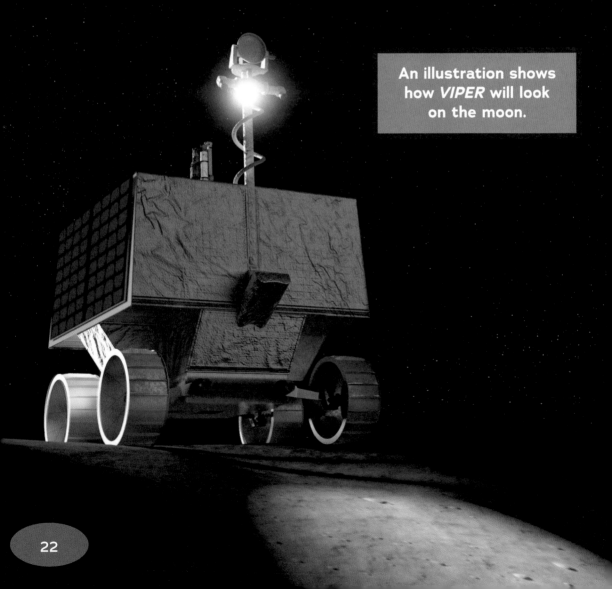

An illustration shows how *VIPER* will look on the moon.

Perhaps comets like this one carried water to the moon.

How did water get on the moon? That's another mystery.

When the moon formed, it was very hot. Any water would have boiled away. But after the moon cooled, comets might have carried water to the moon. Comets are balls of ice and dust that orbit the sun. When comets crashed into the moon, their ice might have mixed in with the soil.

Space scientists study
fossils in Australia.

Mystery in the Rocks

The moon may contain clues about life on Earth. Life
first appeared on our planet around four billion years ago.
Scientists want to find out how life on Earth began. They
often study ancient living things by examining fossils. But
over billions of years, wind and rain have destroyed the
fossil remains of the first living things on Earth.

The earliest fossils might be gone from Earth, but maybe some of them are on the moon. When life was beginning on Earth, many asteroids and comets smashed into our planet. When they hit, they tossed big chunks of rock and soil into space. Maybe some of this material landed on the moon. Maybe it contained fossils. Because the moon has no rain or wind to destroy fossils, maybe some of them are still there.

Scientists think the moon might contain fossils from Earth.

So far, scientists have not found any evidence of life on
the moon. But maybe new moon missions will find fossils
from ancient Earth.

STEM Spotlight

The *VIPER* lunar rover is the size of a golf cart. It is loaded with scientific instruments. It has a drill to take samples of the soil and other tools to test the soil for water. If *VIPER* finds a lot of ice, astronauts might use the ice to set up a moon colony. They could melt the ice to make drinking water. They could use oxygen in the ice to make breathable air. They could make hydrogen from the ice and burn the hydrogen to run machines and heat shelters.

To find answers to the many mysteries of the moon, people will need to go back there. NASA wants to send more people to the moon by 2024. Future astronauts could help uncover some of the moon's biggest secrets.

NASA IS TESTING A NEW MOON ROVER IN THE DESERT IN ARIZONA.

▼

3D Printer Activity

The near side of the moon is much smoother than the far side. To see the difference up close, you can make 3D-printed models of the moon's surface. Follow the below link to download the 3D printer files.

PAGE PLUS

https://qrs.lernerbooks.com/Moon

Glossary

asteroid: a small rocky object that orbits our sun or another star

axis: an imaginary line that runs between the north and south poles of a planet, moon, or other body in space. The space object spins around this line.

comet: a ball of ice and dust that orbits the sun or another star

crust: the hard outer layer of a rocky planet or moon

debris: the remains of something that has been broken or destroyed

fossil: a mark or the remains of something that lived thousands or millions of years ago. An example is animal tracks left in mud that has turned to stone.

gravity: a force that pulls two objects toward each other. The force of gravity pulls things toward the ground.

lava: melted rock that oozes or shoots out of volcanoes and then hardens into rocks

orbit: to travel in a circle around a moon, a planet, or a star

oxygen: a colorless, odorless gas that people and animals need to breathe

seismograph: a device that measures and records vibrations in the ground

Learn More about the Moon

Books

Floca, Brian. *Moonshot: The Flight of Apollo 11.* New York: Atheneum Books for Young Readers, 2019.
This book tells the story of the first time astronauts walked on the moon, on July 20, 1969.

Olson, Elsie. *Breakthroughs in Moon Exploration.* Minneapolis: Lerner Publications, 2020.
Read all about the moon, its human explorers, and plans for future missions.

Slade, Suzanne. *Daring Dozen: The Twelve Who Walked on the Moon.* Watertown, MA: Charlesbridge, 2019.
Meet the twelve American astronauts who walked on the moon.

Websites

NASA Science: Earth's Moon
https://solarsystem.nasa.gov/moons/earths-moon/overview/
Get facts about the only place beyond Earth where people have walked. You can click on a map of the moon to see all places spacecraft have landed.

NASA Space Place: All about the Moon
https://spaceplace.nasa.gov/all-about-the-moon/en/
You'll find fun facts about the moon, along with diagrams and photos.

National Geographic Kids: Facts about the Moon
https://www.natgeokids.com/au/discover/science/space/facts-about-the-moon/
Discover ten fascinating facts about Earth's only moon.

Index

Photo Acknowledgments

Image credits: Henglein and Steets/Cultura/Getty Images, p. 4; NASA/JSC, pp. 5, 9, 11, 13, 14, 17, 20, 26, 27, 29; NASA/GSFC, pp. 6, 16; Flora Stefani/EyeEm/Getty Images, p. 7; Andrew Fare/Alamy Stock Photo, p. 8; China National Space Administration/AFP/Getty Images, p. 10; Stocktrek Images/Getty Images, p. 12; Laura Westlund/Independent Picture Service, pp. 15, 19; Albert Garnelis/TASS/Getty Images, p. 18; aravind chandramohanan/Alamy Stock Photo, p. 21; NASA/ARC/Daniel Rutter, p. 22; NASA/JPL-Caltech/UCLA, p. 23; NASA/JPL-Caltech, p. 24; Kiyomi Yoshimatsu/500px/Getty Images, p. 25; NASA, p. 28.

Cover: SCIEPRO/SCIENCE PHOTO LIBRARY/Getty Images.